# *T*HE WORLD

## MAVIS BATEY

**W**onderland was invented by Lewis Carroll, whose real name was Charles Dodgson. He was a reserved bachelor Oxford don who had a unique gift for telling stories to children – stories that captured for everybody the wonder of childhood and its 'happy summer days'. Dodgson was a great lover of children, and had a deep understanding of their minds and appreciation of their points of view. This stemmed from his own childhood experiences and memories. A great number of his stories have been lost, but Alice Liddell, the daughter of the Dean of Christ Church, insisted that those he told to her and her sisters on a 'golden afternoon' in the summer of 1862 should be written down.

When they were published, *Alice's Adventures in Wonderland* became immortalised, and these were followed by the sequel *Through the Looking-Glass*. The stories have since become known and loved by children and adults all over the world. The tale of how they came to be written is, in many ways, just as fascinating as the *Alice* stories themselves.

*ABOVE LEFT: Alice Liddell, photographed by Charles Dodgson when she was an 'entirely fascinating little seven-year-old maiden'.*

*ABOVE RIGHT: The Lewis Carroll Biscuit Tin, issued in 1892 by Jacobs the biscuit-makers, and made by Hudson of Carlisle. Dodgson supervised it himself and ordered 300 for child friends.*

## THE AUTHOR

Mavis Batey has a flair for literature and a sense of place. Her most recent book was *Jane Austen and the English Landscape*. She became captivated by the background to the *Alice* books when her husband was Treasurer of Christ Church, Oxford, with rooms overlooking the Deanery garden.

# *T*HE BIRTH OF WONDERLAND

Wonderland, a place where exciting stories were made out of everyday events, was first conceived at Charles Dodgson's birthplace, Daresbury in Cheshire, where his father the Reverend Charles Dodgson was the incumbent. The future Lewis Carroll was born in 1832, the third of 11 children, and the eldest son. It was a poor living for the large family, and the parsonage was so remotely situated, in the middle of open fields, that a passing farm cart was an 'event' for the children. Charles's contribution to helping his overworked mother run the household was to entertain his brothers and sisters.

*ABOVE LEFT: Silhouette of Charles Dodgson, aged eight, made at an exhibition in Warrington.*

*ABOVE: The Parsonage at Daresbury, the site of which was bought and laid out as a memorial by the Lewis Carroll Birthplace Trust in 1993.*

*RIGHT: A jigsaw puzzle from the Daresbury nursery.*

The house burned down in 1883, long after the Dodgsons had left, but in 1974 the Lewis Carroll Society marked the spot with an inscription from Carroll's poem 'The Three Sunsets', describing his birthplace:

*An island farm mid seas of corn*
*Swayed by the wandering breath of morn*
*The happy spot where I was born.*

The site of the parsonage was subsequently purchased in 1993 by the Lewis Carroll Birthplace Trust.

*ABOVE, LEFT AND BELOW: Ideas for Wonderland and its animated animal characters were born in Daresbury. It is therefore fitting that the memorial window to Charles Dodgson in All Saints Church, Daresbury, where his father was perpetual curate from 1827 to 1843, should celebrate some of his whimsical creatures.*

# CHILDREN OF THE NORTH

## RIPON CATHEDRAL

ABOVE: *Griffin chasing a rabbit. Carving on the mayor's stall in Ripon Cathedral.*

The Reverend Charles Dodgson, who had been chaplain to the Bishop of Ripon since 1843, was made a Canon of Ripon Cathedral in 1852 and required to reside there for the first three months of the year. His son Charles spent part of his Christmas vacations at Ripon, and from 1862 until his father's death in 1868 continued writing the *Alice* books there at the same time as working on his mathematics. He had been fascinated by the carvings in his father's churches at Daresbury and Croft, and would greatly have enjoyed the famous Ripon misericords, many depicting animated creatures. Alice also imagined carvings coming to life, and used to pretend that the carved lions on the Christ Church Deanery staircase chased her.

Charles Dodgson was very proud of being descended from two ancient northern families who had served their country well. His father's worth at Daresbury was rewarded in 1843 by a much better living at Croft in Yorkshire; this meant a much more spacious house in the centre of the village which gave the 11-year-old Charles more scope for inventive stories and entertainment for the family. He was infatuated with nearby Darlington, the home of Stephenson's Locomotion, and invented the Dodgson railway game in the rectory garden. He made a marionette theatre and toys for his sisters and developed conjuring and puzzle-making skills. He began to illustrate sketches and poems in family magazines, where seeds of the later Wonderland stories appear; these continued in school and college vacations.

While staying with his Wilcox cousins at Whitburn, near Sunderland, in 1855, Charles Dodgson composed the 'Jabberwocky' poem with its famous first verse, which was included in his family magazine 'Mischmash' as a 'stanza of Anglo-Saxon poetry'. Dodgson was very familiar with north-country legends with their *Beowulf* background, where dragons are called 'worms'. An annual ceremony took place on the bridge at Croft, a reminder of the slaying of the Sockburn worm which had long ago terrorised the district; nearer to Whitburn were other legendary monsters, the Lambton Worm and the Laidley Worm.

The Whitburn beach had 'quantities of sand' and oysters, and nearby Sunderland was full of ships' carpenters, and it is probably here that 'The Walrus and the Carpenter', a poem later included in *Through the Looking-Glass*, was conceived.

4

# JABBERWOCKY

Dodgson's nephew, Stuart Dodgson Collingwood, said that it was at Whitburn, while Dodgson was visiting his cousins, that 'to while away an evening, the whole party sat down to a game of verse-making and "Jabberwocky" was his uncle's contribution'. The poem was eventually included in *Through the Looking-Glass*, in a 'Looking-glass book' that Alice had to hold up to the mirror in order to read the writing.

LEFT: *The Jabberwock 'whiffling through the tulgey wood'.*

OPPOSITE : *A family group photograph taken by Charles Dodgson at Croft Rectory in 1857, showing his younger brother Edwin and six of his sisters. Charles felt responsible for his unmarried sisters after their father's death in 1868, and brought them down south to Guildford to be nearer him.*

'Twas brillig, and the slithy toves
    Did gyre and gimble in the wabe;
All mimsy were the borogoves,
    And the mome raths outgrabe.

"Beware the Jabberwock, my son!
    The jaws that bite, the claws that catch!
Beware the Jubjub bird and shun
    The frumious Bandersnatch!"

He took his vorpal sword in hand:
    Long time the manxome foe he sought—
So rested he by the Tumtum tree,
    And stood awhile in thought.

And as in uffish thought he stood,
    The Jabberwock, with eyes of flame,
Came whiffling through the tulgey wood,
    And burbled as it came!

One, two! One, two! And through and through
    The vorpal blade went snicker-snack!
He left it dead, and with its head
    He went galumphing back.

BELOW: *Walrus and Carpenter. Tenniel illustrates the box-like headdress worn by the Sunderland ships' carpenters. The Sunderland Museum now has its own stuffed walrus.*

# LIFE AT CHRIST CHURCH

Charles Dodgson arrived at Christ Church, Oxford, as an undergraduate in 1851 and, except for vacations, remained there for the rest of his life. He was nominated to a Studentship (the equivalent of a fellowship in other colleges) in 1852, attained a first-class degree in mathematics in 1854, was ordained deacon in 1861, and for nine years, from 1882, was Curator of the Common Room. The House, as the cathedral college, or *Aedes Christi*, is known in Oxford, was both home and a way of life for Dodgson for 47 years.

Dodgson was always happiest and most relaxed in the company of children. His rooms were said to resemble a toy shop, but he was extremely tidy and methodical, making sure that slide rules and musical boxes never became muddled up. 'Don't children ever bore you?' asked an incredulous undergraduate. 'Little children are three-fourths of my life; I don't see how they could bore anyone', was the don's sincere reply.

Thomas Fowler, a college friend, later recalled how on a summer vacation trip to Whitby, Yorkshire, in 1854 Dodgson sat on a rock on the beach telling stories to a circle of eager young listeners. Eleven years later, when *Alice's Adventures in Wonderland* was published, Fowler, the future Oxford Professor of Logic, recognised the whimsical fun of the school in the sea, where the master was an old turtle called 'Tortoise', because he 'taught us', and lessons 'lessened' every day until there had to be a day off, and he consequently told people in Oxford that it was at Whitby that the *Alice* stories were first told.

ABOVE: *Mock Turtle. The old schoolmaster turtle was called 'Tortoise' because he 'taught us'.*

RIGHT: *'The Deanery Garden' by J.M.W. Turner. Charles Dodgson first met the Liddell children while they were playing in the shadow of their father's cathedral in 1856.*

# THE DEAN'S DAUGHTER

LEFT: 'Three Daughters of Dean Liddell', 1864, by William Blake Richmond. Alice is seated on the right. Dodgson thought that Alice looked very lovely, 'but not quite natural'. The background is Great Orme's Head, Llandudno.

ABOVE: Penmorfa, the Liddells' holiday house (now the Gogarth Hotel). The Richmond painting was made in the setting of the Liddells' house, first occupied in 1865.

Alice Liddell was born on 4 May 1852 at Westminster School, where her father, the Reverend Henry George Liddell, was headmaster. Alice was four years old when the Liddells moved to the Christ Church Deanery in 1856. The rest of the family consisted of Alice's mother, Lorina (née Reeve), Harry, aged nine, Lorina, six, and Edith, two. Soon after their arrival, Charles Dodgson was given permission to photograph the cathedral from the Deanery garden. Alice and her two sisters immediately came up to him, wanting to be photographed. Dodgson marked the day in his diary with the words 'white stone', a term he reserved for occasions which he felt had significance in his life – the subject of this particular entry was to change his life for ever.

Dodgson's friendship with the Liddell children developed rapidly. He took Harry rowing, and was soon asked to tutor him in mathematics. The little girls, who were taken over to his rooms by their nurse, liked to sit on the sofa and tell 'Mr Dodgson' what they had been doing, so that the events could be turned into Wonderland adventures. Stories about the seaside would have been told from his own repertoire after Alice's excitement over her first visit to the seaside, at Llandudno, in 1861.

# TELL US A STORY

Although child play and mathematics had to be kept apart, there was no personality split between Dodgson the don and Carroll the inventor of fairy tales. A delight in make-believe may seem inconsistent with a logical mind, but Dodgson's imaginative genius was a unique brand of fun-loving nonsense based on logic which appealed instantly to children – especially to an observant, inquiring child like Alice. One child recalled how 'Mr Dodgson' took delight in the absurdity of the misuse of words, and loved to lead children through complicated mazes of reasoning to show that they had actually meant the opposite of what they had said. Alice, who was adept at asking disconcerting questions, enjoyed such teasing.

The exchange between Alice and the Frog Footman in *Through the Looking-Glass* is an example of the nonsense based on wordplay that delighted both the child and the logician:

> *"Where's the servant whose business it is to answer the door?" she began . . . "To answer the door?" he said. "What's it been asking of?"*

*BELOW: The Mad Tea-Party. The text subtly reveals that the date of the party was 4 May, Alice's birthday. Charles Dodgson remembered the date in his diary long after Alice had grown up.*

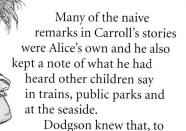

Many of the naive remarks in Carroll's stories were Alice's own and he also kept a note of what he had heard other children say in trains, public parks and at the seaside.

Dodgson knew that, to capture a child's wholehearted attention, the child must be placed at the centre of the story. *Alice's Adventures in Wonderland* begins with the word 'Alice', and Alice is the unmistakable heroine present on every page 'as large as life and twice as natural'. The stories that he told to all the Ediths, Olives, Beatrices and Ruths, although not written down, became each child's own prized possession, treasured all the more in large Victorian families where everything had to be shared. One child recalled that 'my adventures as told by Mr Dodgson made me quite a heroine, and I felt myself a person of some importance with a history'.

Although his stories would take the child into realms of fancy, they would start in familiar surroundings and recall recent actual events in the child's life. From this safe foundation, Dodgson could follow the child's imagination and lead it spellbound into unexpected adventures, as he himself describes in one of the verses preceding the first chapter of *Alice's Adventures in Wonderland*:

> Anon, to sudden silence won
> In fancy they pursue
> The dream-child moving through a land
> Of wonders wild and new,
> In friendly chat with bird or beast ——
> And half believe it true.

*ABOVE: Frog Footman. Alice demands imperiously to have the door opened – it is clearly the Norman door of her father's Chapter House at Christ Church. Charles Dodgson's rooms, where he told his stories, were nearby.*

*TOP LEFT AND LEFT: Dodgson made up stories about things that he and Alice saw together at Christ Church and around Oxford. The brass firedogs in the fireplaces in the Hall may have inspired the illustration of Alice with 'an immense length of neck, which seemed to rise like a stalk'.*

# ALICE'S OXFORD

Walks were a necessary part of the children's afternoon routine, since it was a strict rule that they should not run about in the quad or make too much noise in their garden. This was under the windows of the college Library, from where Dodgson often watched them playing and making daisy chains. They were taken to let off steam in Christ Church Meadow and were delighted when Mr Dodgson was free from his mathematics and could accompany them along the Broad Walk to the Botanic Garden, or take them to see the deer at Magdalen or feed the ducks on Worcester Lake.

Throughout their years at the Deanery, the Liddell children took a lively interest in all that went on in Oxford. Their father's Greek dictionary was a bestseller and in 1863 Dodgson took them round the University Press to see it being set up for its sixth edition. The building of the new University Museum and the laying out of its exhibits was of great interest; the remains of the extinct Dodo, which was to have a new lease of life in Wonderland, fascinated them. Alice couldn't help questioning the need for such erudite classifications of the insects, however, when 'what she really wanted to know was whether it could sting or not'.

*BELOW: The Library. Charles Dodgson was sub-librarian from 1855 to 1857, and worked in a room overlooking the Deanery garden. Alice's cat Dinah sometimes had to be retrieved from the Library.*

Alice knew most of the Oxford professors, since they were the only resident members of the University, other than Heads of Houses and canons of Christ Church, who were allowed to marry, and most of her friends were professors' children. She was very familiar with academics who talked like the eggheaded professor Humpty Dumpty or were ready to give philosophical advice like the hookah-smoking Caterpillar. Professor Bartholomew Price, who was a great friend and former tutor of Dodgson, was well known at the Deanery. He was always known as 'Bat' in Oxford, as he had a habit of flying over everybody's heads in his lectures, which Dodgson conveniently linked with his interest in astronomy for Alice's Wonderland:

> *Twinkle, twinkle, little bat!*
> *How I wonder what you're at!*
> *Up above the world you fly,*
> *Like a tea-tray in the sky!*

# BINSEY AND THE TREACLE WELL

Alice knew well the village of Binsey, by the Thames, as her governess's family lived there, and on fine days Miss Prickett would sometimes take the children along the towpath to visit them. St Frideswide's holy well at Binsey has a special connection with both Oxford and Wonderland. Alice had been brought up on the story of Oxford's patron saint, in whose honour her father preached the St Frideswide sermon each year on her festival, 19 October. The saint's shrine is in Christ Church Cathedral, which is built on the site of the monastery she founded, and in 1860 a St Frideswide's window, commissioned by Dean Liddell and painted by Sir Edward Burne-Jones, was dedicated.

All Christ Church had watched the glass panels, showing scenes in the Saxon princess's life, being assembled on the grass behind the Latin chapel. One of the panels portrayed the Binsey holy well, with a signpost that read 'Oxford-Binsey' linking the two places of pilgrimage in the Middle Ages. It is said that St Frideswide was pursued to Binsey by King Algar, who wanted to marry her but was struck blind for his boldness. Her prayers to St Margaret called forth a miraculous well whose waters cured her suitor's blindness, and he departed thankfully, leaving her to return to Oxford and found her monastery in peace. The holy well became known as the Treacle Well in Binsey, the word 'treacle' being used in its medieval sense of a healing fluid.

*OPPOSITE: St Frideswide's Window, Christ Church Cathedral, by Burne-Jones. The Binsey Treacle Well features in one of the scenes.*

*BELOW: Alice's governess's family, the Pricketts, lived at Binsey, near the Thames.*

The well had long since become overgrown, but in 1857 Dodgson's friend the Reverend Thomas Prout had decided to clear it when he became incumbent of the church. This happened in time for it to appear in Wonderland, during the Mad Tea Party:

> "Once upon a time there were three little sisters," the Dormouse began in a great hurry; "and their names were Elsie, Lacie, and Tillie; and they lived at the bottom of a well —"

Elsie was Lorina Charlotte (LC), Lacie was Alice, and Tillie was Edith's pet name. When Alice, rather naturally, asked the Dormouse why these three little girls should live at the bottom of a well, she was told it was a 'treacle-well'. Alice was beginning to say that there was no such thing, but then she remembered that there might be *one* after all.

# CAMERAS AND COSTUMES

OPPOSITE: *The Queen's croquet ground. The cards have fallen flat on their faces at the approach of the Queen of Hearts. The Oxford Botanic Garden waterlily house can be seen in the background.*

Amateur photography became very popular in 1851 when the collodion process was developed (collodion was a chemical solution used for developing the plates). Dodgson, who acquired his first camera in 1856, soon became accomplished, and would have made his name as a Victorian photographer if he had not become famous as the writer Lewis Carroll.

Being able to record the likenesses of his child friends at special moments was a great delight, for, as he said, they would 'grow up so quick'. Many are of Alice, taken so that he could remember his 'dream-child' as 'an entirely fascinating little seven-year-old maiden'. Child friends remembered how the smell of collodion hung about Dodgson's rooms. Alice recalled that, despite having to sit still for so long in those early days of amateur photography, having their pictures taken was not boring for her and her sisters, as it went hand in hand with story-telling of a special kind.

Dodgson kept a dressing-up cupboard which included a Turkish costume, a fairy prince outfit and a suit of mail. He had a flair for unobtrusive instruction, which although common in every nursery school today was unheard of in the 1860s. Before Alice and Lorina dressed up in Chinese costume, Dodgson would have talked to them about the geography and customs of China. Macartney's famous *Embassy to China*, which Dodgson could have borrowed from Christ Church library, was the best-illustrated book of travels to China. Much is made in this book of the visit to the Emperor, who was borne aloft on a gold palanquin, and before him everybody had to kowtow. When he appeared, Macartney wrote, 'Instantly the whole court fell flat on their faces'. In *Alice's*

ABOVE: *Alice (seated) and Lorina, photographed by Dodgson. Their Chinese costumes were probably borrowed from the Ashmolean Museum.*

*Below:* Tom Tower. When Charles Dodgson had rooms in the north-west corner of Tom Quad, he used to let children play hide-and-seek among the chimney stacks on the roof. Christopher Wren's tower houses the great bell, Tom, brought from Osney Abbey. The sound of the bell is a familiar one in Oxford. The lion in Through the Looking-Glass *speaks 'in a deep hollow tone that sounded like the tolling of a great bell'.*

*Adventures in Wonderland*, the imperious Queen of Hearts, with her crown borne before her, orders the cards to prostrate themselves. Tenniel's illustration shows, in the right foreground, how 'the three gardeners instantly threw themselves flat on their faces'. What the storybook Alice said must surely be what the real Alice would have said of Macartney's Emperor, with all the logic of a seven-year-old:

> ". . . what would be the use of a procession", thought she, "if people had all to lie down upon their faces, so that they couldn't see it?"

15

# THE GOLDEN AFTERNOON

Special treats for Edith, Lorina and Alice, marked with a 'white stone' in Dodgson's diary, were their boating trips on the Thames, or the Isis as it is called in Oxford. Dodgson would ask one of his friends to come with them, usually the Reverend Robinson Duckworth of Trinity, who was famous for his renderings of popular songs. Perhaps because there was no governess to supervise the children, the party was always relaxed.

On 4 July 1862, a memorable excursion took place, this time up the river to Godstow, passing Binsey on the way. As they rowed upstream from Salter's boat yard opposite Christ Church, Dodgson picked up the threads of the never-ending story of Alice's adventures, in which Alice was the heroine, her sisters Lorina and Edith were the Lory and the Eaglet, Duckworth was the Duck, and Dodgson was the Dodo. The story began with Alice going down a rabbit hole and, 'owing to the frequent interruptions', as Alice recalled, 'fresh and undreamed-of possibilities' opened up.

They had a picnic at Godstow on farmland, next to a backwater of the Thames where there were some eel

*ABOVE: Charles Dodgson identified himself as the Dodo, who can be seen to be wearing an academic sleeve. The Duck was his friend Duckworth. The monkey is very relevant, as the famous evolution debate was held at Oxford in 1860, when the heated Darwinite Thomas Huxley told Bishop Wilberforce that he would rather be descended from a monkey than a bishop. Dodgson took a photograph of Huxley afterwards. The Darwinist Professor Daubeny kept monkeys in the Botanic Garden.*

*RIGHT: The picnic on the river on the 'golden afternoon' took place by the river at Godstow.*

traps – inspiring the poem about 'Father William' who balanced an eel on his nose, as well as standing on his head and performing somersaults. Balancing and somersaulting were very much on the children's minds, as a few days earlier they had been taken to see the great French acrobat Blondin demonstrate on a low rope in Oxford the feats he had performed over the Niagara Falls in Canada.

The children waited for more stories as they were rowing back, but Dodgson, who was by then a little weary, said 'That's all till next time'. 'Ah, but it *is* next time', they cried, and with some persuasion Alice's adventures were started up again. His stories normally 'lived and died like summer midges', in Dodgson's own words, but this time it was different; when Alice bade her friends goodnight on the Deanery doorstep, she said 'Oh, Mr Dodgson, I wish you would write out Alice's adventures for me'.

According to Duckworth, Dodgson sat up nearly all night writing down what he could remember. Everything he undertook was done to perfection, however, and it was not until two years later, at the end of 1864, that Alice received the finished version of 'Alice's Adventures Under Ground', inscribed as 'A Christmas Gift to a Dear Child in Memory of a Summer Day'.

*ABOVE: Father William. Alice would have seen eels in the wicker traps by the Godstow weir.*

♥

In the poem that precedes the beginning of *Alice's Adventures in Wonderland*, Dodgson recalls the events of that memorable day. Three of the verses read as follows.

All in the golden afternoon
    Full leisurely we glide;
For both our oars, with little skill,
    By little arms are plied,
While little hands make vain pretence
    Our wanderings to guide.

Ah, cruel Three! In such an hour,
    Beneath such dreamy weather,
To beg a tale of breath too weak
    To stir the tiniest feather!
Yet what can one poor voice avail
    Against three tongues together?

Thus grew the tale of Wonderland:
    Thus slowly, one by one,
Its quaint events were hammered out—
    And now the tale is done,
And home we steer, a merry crew
    Beneath the setting sun.

# W HAT IS THE USE OF A BOOK WITHOUT PICTURES?

No 1.
A 13

*RIGHT: The Mouse's tail as pasted up by Dodgson as a guide for the printer.*

Fury said to a mouse, That he met in the house, "Let us both go to law : I will prosecute you. Come, I'll take no denial ; We must have a trial : For really this morning I've nothing to do," Said the mouse to the cur, "Such a trial, dear sir, With no jury or judge, would be wasting our breath." "I'll be judge, I'll be jury," Said cunning old Fury : "I'll try the whole cause, and condemn you to death."

*ABOVE: Charles Dodgson's meticulous instructions to Macmillan for inserting illustrations into the text of* Alice's Adventures in Wonderland.

Friends who saw the delightful manuscript book that Dodgson was creating for Alice urged him to publish it. At first, however, he was unwilling to believe that the stories about Alice and her sisters, interspersed with the songs, games and jokes they had shared, would be of general interest. His friend George Macdonald, a children's writer, tried it out on his son, who was so enthusiastic that he 'wished there were 60,000 volumes of it'.

'What is the use of a book without pictures?' is the question asked by Alice at the very beginning of her adventures, about the book her sister was reading, when the White Rabbit suddenly runs past and the story begins. Dodgson was well aware of the importance of illustrations, and initially he hoped that if he took instruction his own drawings could be used in the published version of the book. His friend John Ruskin, the eminent art critic and author, advised him that his talent was not sufficient to merit devoting much time to it, however.

Early in 1864, when Dodgson had resigned himself to finding a professional illustrator, it was arranged for him to meet John Tenniel, whose *Punch* illustrations Dodgson greatly admired. There could have been no better choice. Indeed it is difficult to think of the *Alice* books without Tenniel's line drawings, so perfectly do they match Dodgson's vision, having just the right note of matter-of-factness to bring the nonsense tales to life.

Dodgson gave the publishers, Macmillan, exact instructions regarding how the illustrations should be inserted in the text. Bill the lizard was to shoot 5 inches up the page, Alice's neck was to grow 5⅛ inches and the Cheshire cat's grin was to be 10 lines high. All was finally agreed, and the first printed copy of *Alice's Adventures in Wonderland* was sent to Alice on 4 July 1865, three years to the day after the 'golden afternoon' which had inspired the book, and only seven months after she had received the manuscript version.

## DODGSON THE ARTIST

Dodgson knew most of the artists of the Pre-Raphaelite
Movement working in Oxford. In 1863, the year he was
drawing the illustrations for Alice's manuscript book, he
received Arthur Hughes' 'Girl with Lilacs', which had
been specially painted for his rooms. The image of his
own heroine, Alice, in the manuscript version, was clearly
influenced by the paintings of both Hughes and Dante
Gabriel Rossetti. What emerges is not the perky little
Alice with the dark brown fringe of the photographs, but
one with a soulful Pre-Raphaelite look and crinkly hair.
Dodgson also borrowed a natural history book from
the Deanery and experimented with draft illustrations of
birds and animals for wood blocks.

ABOVE: *Dodgson's original manuscript
drawing of Alice. He was unhappy with it,
and pasted a photograph of her over the
drawing. The illustration was later
uncovered by the British Library.*

FAR LEFT: *'Girl
with Lilacs'.
Hughes' painting
can be seen to the
right of the
chimneypiece in
Dodgson's sitting
room (see page 6).*

LEFT: *Dodgson's
own drawing of
Alice with crinkly
Pre-Raphaelite
hair and a
soulful look.*

# *L*OOKING-GLASS HOUSE

Alice's adventures, so long as she and her don friend were together, continued as an 'interminable fairy-tale' even after she achieved her ambition that 'there ought to be a book written about me, that there ought'. The year 1863 saw Dodgson arranging for the publication of Alice's adventures as inspired by the 'golden afternoon' of 1862, and was a time of special closeness between him and the Liddell children, inspiring renewed bouts of story-telling. These later stories, however, were not written down at the time, and remained in Dodgson's head.

Mrs Liddell was expecting a baby at the end of March 1863, and the children were sent away to the Dean's mother at Hetton Lawn, Charlton Kings, near Cheltenham, with their governess. Dodgson spent the Easter vacation with friends at Tenby, Wales, and was pleased to receive an invitation to break his return journey to Oxford at Cheltenham. Alice's visit to her grandmother's house, with the great looking-glass mirror over the drawing-room mantelpiece, was to play an important part in the new book, to be called *Through the Looking-Glass*.

*BELOW: Alice going through the looking glass at Hetton Lawn, her grandmother's house near Cheltenham, from the lid of the 1892 Biscuit Box (see page 1).*

ALICE THROUGH THE LOOKING GLASS

By kind permission of the Author LEWIS CARROLL.

As we know from *Alice's Adventures in Wonderland*, those present when the story was told often appeared as characters. Undoubtedly, the governess, Miss Prickett, who was with the children all the time at Hetton Lawn, became the Red Queen. The children called her 'Pricks', and in the 'Garden of Live Flowers' it is said of the Red Queen that 'she's one of the thorny kind'. Tenniel certainly manages to make the Red Queen look rather fierce and spiky when she is wagging her finger at Alice. This probably reflects a real event on the breezy walk they all took up Leckhampton Hill, above the Gloucestershire plain which Alice thought was laid out like a large chess-board.

Dodgson travelled back to Oxford with the children on a hilarious journey where the train 'jumped over six little brooks', an incident also recalled in the pages of *Through the Looking-Glass*. When they got back to the Deanery, the children found they had a new baby brother.

It was not until August 1866 that Dodgson told Macmillan that he had 'a floating idea of writing a sort of sequel to *Alice*'. For the second book Dodgson wrote with publication in mind. The story is consequently more sophisticated, with its chess-game setting, and inevitably more nostalgic. Alice was 19 years old, and had long since ceased to beg for stories, when *Through the Looking-Glass* was finally published in 1871.

**ABOVE:** *The view from Leckhampton Hill over the Gloucester Plain. Dodgson recorded in his diary: 'Except for the high wind, the day could hardly have been better for the view; the children were in the wildest spirits.'*

**LEFT:** *Red Queen and Alice. In his instructions for 'Alice' on the stage, Dodgson said that the Red Queen was the 'concentrated essence of all governesses'. As the Red Queen, 'Pricks', the Liddell children's governess, is shown to be 'one of the thorny kind'.*

**BELOW:** *Tenniel's illustration of the landscape marked out just like a 'large chess-board'.*

# KINGS AND QUEENS

'Let's pretend we're kings and queens', said Alice, near the beginning of *Through the Looking-Glass*. Real royals, as well as the playing cards and chess pieces, had played a recognizable part in Alice's life. Queen Victoria decided to place Edward, Prince of Wales, under the Dean's specific charge while Edward was attending Oxford.

*BELOW: The royal banquet with the Christ Church ceremonial plate. When Alice cries 'I can't stand this any longer', and pulls the tablecloth off the High Table, the port decanters mysteriously acquire wings and presumably find their way back to the Common Room.*

*ABOVE RIGHT: 'An invitation from the Queen to play croquet'.*

Although the Prince had his own establishment at Frewen Hall, he made frequent visits to the Deanery, where the hour for dinner was changed to suit him. He sometimes went to the children's drawing-room performances, and enjoyed teasing Alice. Dodgson presented the Prince with some of his photographs of the children. A special banquet was given in Hall for the Prince's 18th birthday, and there was traditional turtle soup on the menu.

The Royal Wedding, between Edward and Princess Alexandra, took place in 1863, the year in which most of the *Looking-Glass* stories were told, and the event was a highlight in Alice's life. Oxford sported spectacular gas illuminations, and Alice toured the city with Dodgson and his brother. Christ Church, as befitted the Royal Foundation and the Prince of Wales's old college, displayed an illumination depicting the Prince's feathers and the initials of

the happy pair on the St Aldates frontage, and a revolving crown of variegated lights over Canterbury gate. The crown is persistently in Alice's thoughts in *Through the Looking-Glass* and much of the imagery of the 'Lion and the Unicorn' chapter relates to these illuminations.

The royal couple spent three days at the Deanery at the end of their honeymoon, and Dodgson photographed the new royal bed with Alice and her sister sitting importantly on the window seat behind. Although there was a packed schedule of receptions, balls, fêtes and an honorary degree ceremony, Princess Alexandra insisted that there should be a croquet engagement with the children in the Deanery garden.

Alice had been told in her fantasy game of chess in *Through the Looking-Glass* that when she became a queen she would have to give a banquet; it turned out to be very like the real Christ Church banquet with protocol, a dressed-up leg of mutton, port decanters and waiting on royal words. In the story, Alice found this rather frightening, and she was also afraid that her crown might fall off. For the real Alice, who was growing up fast, it was the end of her adventures in Wonderland and Looking-Glass land, and she would soon part company with her don friend.

*ABOVE: When Princess Alexandra presented prizes to the University Volunteers in Tom Quad on 16 June 1863, the Liddell children were on the dais (this picture appeared in the* Illustrated London News*).*

*LEFT: Leg of Mutton. 'It isn't etiquette to cut anyone you've been introduced to.' The humour in* Through the Looking-Glass *is much more* Punch*-like than in the first, more naive, Alice* book.

*LEFT: Wolsey's great kitchen at Christ Church. When turtle soup was on the menu, Christ Church children were allowed to ride on the live turtles around the kitchen before the 'beautiful soup' was made. There are still turtle shells on the wall.*

# THE WHITE KNIGHT'S FAREWELL

When Dodgson came to assemble the material for *Through the Looking-Glass*, and check it with his diary, he realised that his last precious excursion with Alice had been to Nuneham park, five miles downstream from Oxford, at the end of the summer term of 1863, when Alice was 11. Nuneham was owned by the uncle of one of Dodgson's friends, Augustus Vernon-Harcourt, and the Harcourts provided picnic huts in the woods. This had always been a favourite full-day river excursion, and one which the 80-year-old Alice later recalled with special pleasure in her *Recollections*:

> To us the hut might have been a Fairy King's palace, and the picnic a banquet in our honour. Sometimes we were told stories after luncheon that transported us into Fairyland.

*ABOVE: Nuneham dingle, the cottages by the river where Dodgson and the children borrowed plates, glasses, knives and forks for their picnics.*

*ABOVE RIGHT: Nuneham park, a fine landscape park by Capability Brown, owned by an uncle of Dodgson's Christ Church friend, Augustus Vernon-Harcourt. It was in the wood on the right that the White Knight said his goodbye to Alice.*

In *Through the Looking-Glass*, in which the character of the White Knight represented Dodgson himself, the author recalls this last precious outing to the woods. The White Knight says to Alice: 'I'll see you safe to the end of the wood – and then I must go back, you know. That's the end of my move.'

There were only casual encounters with Alice after this. The child was growing up, and the magic and the rapport were ending. The White Knight's retrospective farewell is, therefore, all the more poignant:

"You've only a few yards to go," he said, "down the hill and over that little brook, and then you'll be a Queen – But you'll stay and see me off first?' he added as Alice turned with an eager look in the direction to which he pointed. "I sha'n't be long. You'll wait and wave your handkerchief when I get to that turn in the road! I think it'll encourage me, you see."

The ideal child friend was to become a dream-child, the epitome of childhood and all that the friendship of children would always mean to Charles Dodgson. It was with deep emotion that he dedicated *Through the Looking-Glass*, finally published in December 1871, to Alice:

Child of the pure unclouded brow
And dreaming eyes of wonder!
Though time be fleet, and I and thou
Are half a life asunder,
Thy loving smile will surely hail
The love-gift of a fairy-tale.

LEFT: *The White Knight. Dodgson saw himself as the chivalrous knight escorting Alice until she grew out of childhood.*

ABOVE: *The last photograph Dodgson took of Alice, in 1870, the year before* Through the Looking-Glass *was published. The magic and the rapport had gone.*

LEFT: *'Sir Isumbras at the Ford'. There is a strong resemblance to the Knight in this painting by Sir John Everett Millais, whom Dodgson had met and admired. Dodgson said Alice 'took in like a picture' the White Knight's 'mild blue eyes and kindly smile' and the 'setting sun gleaming through his hair'.*

25

ABOVE: *Christ Church from the river, by J.M.W. Turner. At the end of 'Alice's Adventures Under Ground' Alice's sister imagines the story being told to generations of children and the imagery lasting for ever: 'She saw an ancient city, and a quiet river winding near it along the plain, and up the stream went slowly gliding a boat with a merry party of children on board – she could hear their voices and laughter like music over the water.' This connection with Oxford was removed from the published version.*

Dodgson continued to see himself in the role of the White Knight, escorting children through to adolescence. All the magic moments shared with children were stored in his mind and, 'ever-drifting down the stream of life', he had instant recall of them. He wrote hundreds of delightful letters to children, each like a miniature Wonderland, and made up games, cyphers and puzzles for them.

Many of his later child friends were those he met on seaside holidays, or child actresses, particularly those who played in the stage productions of 'Alice'. In the 1880s, dons were finally allowed to marry, and North Oxford was full of children, who could be taken for walks by Dodgson in the University parks and on his special Oxford tours, ending up with tea and cakes in his rooms.

The *Alice* books were never far from Dodgson's mind, and each new edition was carefully checked. He shrank from the publicity that acknowledged authorship would have brought him. Any letters addressed to Lewis Carroll, Christ Church, would be returned to the Post Office marked 'not known'.

The Bodleian Library received a sharp rebuke for a catalogue entry linking Charles Dodgson the author of *An Elementary Treatise on Determinants* with Lewis Carroll the author of *Alice's Adventures in Wonderland*. Many people in Oxford did know his secret, of course, and eagerly awaited fresh masterpieces. 'No it is not funny – it's about Euclid,' was the firm reply Dodgson gave to a lady who called on him while he was engrossed in writing a new book.

In 1880, Alice married Reginald Hargreaves, and in 1885 Dodgson wrote to her, at Lyndhurst, to seek her permission to publish a facsimile of the original 'Alice's Adventures Under Ground', which was still in her possession. 'I have had scores of child friends since your time,' he wrote, 'but they have been quite a different thing.' Dodgson's old friend the Reverend Duckworth (the Duck) was one of the first to receive a copy of the facsimile, published in 1886, inscribed 'The Duck from the Dodo'. Alice's copy, bound in white vellum, said it all, over 20 years after the 'golden afternoon':

> *To Her whose namesake one happy summer day inspired this story.*

LEFT AND ABOVE: *Tenniel's illustration for 'He's an Anglo-Saxon Messenger – and those are Anglo-Saxon attitudes' was based on the Caedmon Genesis*, c. AD *1000, in the Bodleian Library, of which Alice's father was a curator. The manuscripts were put on public display in 1863 in time to feature in* Through the Looking-Glass.

# Not for Money and Not for Fame

## THE MEMORIAL PLAQUE AT CROFT

### LEWIS CARROLL
#### 1832–1898
WAS THE ELDEST SON OF
THE VENERABLE CHARLES DODGSON
RECTOR OF CROFT
AND ARCHDEACON OF RICHMOND
1843–1868

HE SPENT HIS BOYHOOD YEARS
AT CROFT RECTORY WHERE SOME
OF HIS EARLY WRITINGS WERE DONE.
FROM A PLAYFUL INVERSION
OF HIS BAPTISMAL NAMES
CHARLES LUTWIDGE
HE FORMED THE PEN NAME
BY WHICH MILLIONS OF CHILDREN
WHO LOVE HIS WORKS
HAVE COME TO KNOW HIM

LESS WIDELY KNOWN
FROM THAT SAME HAND
COME THESE NOSTALGIC LINES

I'd give all wealth that years have piled,
the slow result of life's decay,
To be once more a little child
for one bright summer day.

Charles Dodgson died in 1898, while spending Christmas with his sisters at their home, The Chestnuts, in Guildford. Alice Hargreaves remembered, all her life, her childhood friendship with the Christ Church mathematics don, just as the White Knight hoped she would do. In 1932, at the age of 80, Alice went to America to celebrate the centenary of his birth, and received an honorary degree at Columbia University for having inspired two great works of literature. Alice's original manuscript was sold to America, but in 1948 it was bought by wellwishers, who gave it to the British Museum as 'an expression of thanks to a noble people who had held Hitler at bay for a long period single-handed'. It was received by the Archbishop of Canterbury, who called the American gesture an 'unsullied and innocent act in a distracted and sinful world'.

Charles Dodgson – Lewis Carroll – wrote his nonsense stories 'not for money, and not for fame, but in the hope of supplying, for the children whom I love, some thoughts that may suit those hours of innocent merriment which are the very life of Childhood: and also in the hope of suggesting to them and to others some thoughts that may prove, I would fain hope, not wholly out of harmony with the graver cadences of life.'

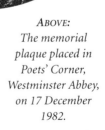

Alice's adventures have continued to delight generations of children and adults all over the world, but as she herself said, on the centenary of his birth, 'I wonder how many stories the world has missed because he never wrote anything down until I teased him into doing it'.

*ABOVE:*
*The memorial plaque placed in Poets' Corner, Westminster Abbey, on 17 December 1982.*